C000164702

THE WAY

'Carl Beech tells great stories; real stories about the ups and downs of trying to walk in Jesus' footsteps through the mess, muddle and bliss of daily life. It will do you good and help you to do more good.'

Graham Kendrick, Singer, Songwriter and Worship Leader

'Carl has long been known for reaching men but his ministry is much broader, and this book on living a grace-filled life will help all of us, men and women, young and older, to reach our neighbours and friends. Well worth reading.'

Mark Melluish, Senior Pastor at St Paul's Ealing, and New Wine London and West Regional Director

'With a steady mix of illuminating storytelling, brutal honesty, wry humour and a love for Scripture, Carl brings some fresh perspectives on some of the most amazing passages in the Bible. A joy to read, a challenge to live, but absolutely compelling for every Christ-follower.'

Matt Summerfield, President of Urban Saints

'Jesus always calls ordinary people with the challenge, "Follow me." Carl shows how sticking close to Christ has the potential to change your mind, change your life, and change the world!'

Anthony Delaney, Church Leader, Speaker, Author and Broadcaster

'I've had the privilege of hearing much of this powerful teaching as Carl road tested it on the team here at The Message Trust. So trust me, it's powerful, life-changing stuff.'

Andy Hawthorne OBE, Evangelist, Author and Founder of The Message Trust

'As Christians we know we should turn the other cheek and live with an opposite spirit to everything the world is telling us. But how on earth do we do this? This book is practical, down to earth, and calls us all to be part of a grace revolution.'

Simon Thomas, Sky Sports Presenter and former Blue Peter Presenter

'Radical, refreshing and a real challenge.'

Lyndon Bowring, Speaker and Executive Chairman of CARE

'Carl carves out a deep, Jesus-centred spirituality, but remains accessible, humorous and outward looking. He shares his life with us in these pages, and leaves the reader warmed, yet challenged; invited in, yet inspired to get out there... a must read!'

**Tania Bright, Speaker, Executive Director of
Church Response For Refugees**

'Carl's style is engaging, humorous and always provocative. When applied, this book will change lives.'

Roy Crowne, Executive Director of HOPE Together

'Rooted in Scripture, this book inspires and exhorts us to seek a new way of life. The transformation of our value system will almost certainly lead us to be transformational in our neighbourhoods and work places.'

Sam Ward, National Director of Eden, The Message Trust

'This book challenged me to think about how I practically respond to people in day-to-day life. A must read for anyone seeking to walk more like Jesus.'

Mark Tate, The Grove Team Leader

'Carl Beech lives the message he preaches. Through sharing his stories he will have you laughing out loud and living out loud as you recapture the heart of what it means to be a follower of 'the way'.'

Tim Alford, National Director of Limitless

'I believe this book could cause a reawakening of grace and Christ-centred living that could be truly transformational'

Debra Green OBE, Founder and National Director of ROC

'Carl Beech takes us on a practical journey out of our comfort zones to live lives that provoke questions and spark conversations. *The Way*, rich in Carl's experiences, shows that following Jesus is not about playing the games of this world but about being a grace-empowered people showing another world is possible.'

Andy Frost, Director of Share Jesus International

Living **the Beatitudes** today

CARL BEECH

CWR

© Carl Beech 2017

Published 2017 by CWR, Waverley Abbey House, Waverley Lane, Farnham, Surrey GU9 8EP, UK. CWR is a Registered Charity – Number 294387 and a Limited Company registered in England – Registration Number 1990308.

The right of Carl Beech to be identified as the author of this work has been asserted by him in accordance with the Copyright, Designs and Patents Act 1988, sections 77 and 78.

All rights reserved. No part of this publication may be reproduced, stored in a retrieval system, or transmitted, in any form or by any means, electronic, mechanical, photocopying, recording or otherwise, without the prior permission in writing of CWR.

For a list of National Distributors, visit www.cwr.org.uk/distributors

All Scripture references are from the Holy Bible: New International Version® Anglicised, NIV® Copyright © 1979, 1984, 2011 by Biblica, Inc.® Used by permission. All rights reserved worldwide.

Concept development, editing, design and production by CWR.

Printed in the UK by Linney.

ISBN: 978-1-78259-733-9

Thanks

Big thanks are due to Lynette Brooks at CWR for working with me again to publish this book. Thanks also to The Message Trust family, who spur me on to pursue Christ with passion and hunger to see lives transformed – particularly thanks to Meg Latham, who painstakingly transcribed several chapters and also Peter Wooding for writing up two amazing testimonies. Hugely appreciated.

I've written this book in the margins of a busy life helping to lead The Message Trust, leading a church, being on various boards etc... so it's been my family who have been impacted most as I tried to pull this project together late at night and in the early hours. Thank you Karen, Emily and Annie for putting up with me tapping away on my keyboard or staring into the distance as I pondered a thought or idea.

Of course, none of this would've happened had I not encountered Christ on 22 April 1990. To me, Jesus is the most remarkable character and leader the world has ever seen and to Him I give all the praise and glory.

Deo optimo maximo.

"'Come, follow me,'
Jesus said'

MATTHEW 4:19

Contents

Foreword

How can we live 'the way' of Christ? How can we bring others to know it for themselves? I love the saying, 'Where work, commitment and pleasure meet, you reach that deep well called passion. Here, anything is possible.' I know very well that it's the passionate people who change the world, not the most gifted or resourced. However, it's clear that passion on its own is never going to get the job done. Alongside passion is also the need to have a desire for purity; the kind of purity that Jesus so beautifully demonstrated and articulated in the Sermon on the Mount.

For a long time, I've appreciated and respected Carl Beech. I have always loved his passion to make the gospel of Jesus front and centre. Our paths crossed many times at Christian festivals and leaders' gatherings, and when he spoke, I would often be the guy at the back with a pen and paper, taking notes to make sure I could steal his best stories!

In the last 18 months, through what can only be described as a series of God interventions, we have started to work closely together and our friendship has deepened. I've now discovered so much more about him. He always came across as an alpha male type, who seemed as if he would like to drink beer and blow up cars; now I know that he likes to paint watercolours, play classical piano and has a penchant for pink champagne! But more than this, I've come to know that he has a real pastor's heart and a genuine desire to see Christians grow in their

Christlikeness. He cares about people and aspires to help them become those who can authentically share Jesus with a hurting world.

Along with the rest of The Message Trust team, I've heard the material in this book at our devotional times over the last months. I know for sure that if we can read, digest and apply it, it truly is explosive stuff.

As Carl explains so clearly and relevantly, Jesus Himself knew that good doctrine, powerful preaching – even lots of that 'passion' stuff – weren't going to get the job done. Alongside these things, we need to get hold of godly, counter-cultural living. This really is the way to the transformation that we all long to see in our lives, and the lives of others. So read on, dig deep and get to the heart of what living 'the way' really means today.

Andy Hawthorne OBE

Introduction

When you encounter Jesus, it can feel like stepping out of a grainy, black and white picture and into a full-colour, HD world. It is the best thing you ever imagined... 'But what now?', you might ask. How do we start and continue to follow Jesus, as He calls us to?

Those who followed the teachings of Jesus in the ancient Middle East were first known as 'Christians' in a place called Antioch. Before then, their lifestyles, character and culture were so radically different and at odds with the Roman world around them, that they were simply known as followers of 'the Way' (see Acts 19:23; 24:14,22 for some examples).

In one sense, to be a follower of the way is beautifully simple. In another, it may take more courage, discipline, self-sacrifice and determination than seems humanly possible. But with God's Spirit at work within us, a radical, counter-cultural life is possible.

For just under 10,000 days (at time of writing), I've been a follower of Christ. In the following chapters, I'm going to attempt to share what has been a deeply personal journey of trying to follow the way of Jesus through how I live out my life. I have stumbled and failed more than I have succeeded, but I believe the Holy Spirit has been, and still is, teaching me.

Why follow 'the way'? Mainly because I love God and all that He's done for me, so I want to! But I also truly believe that if all followers of Christ everywhere were determined to put into practical action the teachings of Jesus, the world we live in would look very different indeed.

The key Bible teaching we will be focusing on is taken from Matthew 5–7 – also famously known as the Sermon on the Mount. Starting with the Beatitudes – blessed are the poor, blessed are the meek, blessed are the peacemakers etc – and then moving on to being the salt and light, honouring one another, going the extra mile, and so on, we will consider how and why Jesus calls us to be and do such things.

I think this is some of the most radical stuff that I've explored and applied to my life. All of this is to do with our heart and character, so it's challenging to the core. I believe we are called to live with an 'opposite spirit' to that of the world and surrounding culture. We are beset with unique challenges in the twenty-first century. The proliferation of social media and the pressures of our 'screen culture' present us with many opportunities to live in such a way that is far from Christlike. I hope that in some small way we are able to be the difference, and that – in some way still – this book might encourage us all to embrace 'the way' and live counter-cultural lives.

If ever there was a time and a need for Christians to shine the light of Christ, it's now.

'Blessed are the poor in spirit,
for theirs is the kingdom of heaven.'

MATTHEW 5:3

'So Abraham called that place
The LORD Will Provide.'

GENESIS 22:14

One

Alive

I ride motorbikes. Mostly for the convenience of traffic avoidance on my daily (and very early) 100-mile-round-trip commute, but in all honesty, riding a bike over the Peaks to Manchester does make me feel a little bit alive too! It gets my heart pumping. But the truth is, nothing has ever made me feel more alive than to live for something that is bigger than me. Nothing has made me feel more alive than living for Christ and His kingdom.

'Blessed are the poor in spirit.' I believe the poor in spirit are those who know that they need God – *really* need Him. And ultimately, it is a matter of life and death.

There is a story in the Bible that is incredibly majestic, yet confusing and even a bit harrowing at the same time. In Genesis 22 we read about Abraham's ultimate test of faith. (If you've never read it or need a refresher, give it a read now.) In short, God tells Abraham to take his beloved son Isaac and sacrifice him on a mountain. Horrific! If you have a child of your own, you probably can't even think about such an act. But Abraham was faithful and he set off to do what was asked of him. When a perplexed Isaac asked about the lack of an animal to sacrifice, Abraham responded with, 'God will provide the lamb'.

Abraham proceeded to bind up his son and place him on the altar. At the last second, when Abraham raised his knife into the air, God called, 'Stop!' A ram appeared and Abraham was instructed to sacrifice it instead. Phew!

Before we get caught up with, 'How could God do this?', we should note that God *did* do this – only He was the Father in the story. I've found about 40 parallels between Abraham's story and the account of Jesus' death. They're quite remarkable. Here are just a few:

- The father leads his son to be sacrificed
- A donkey is involved on the road to sacrifice
- The son is the one and only son (and the Bible says so numerous times)

- The son carried the wood to the place of sacrifice
- The son was submissive to the will of the father
- The father loves the son
- The Lord himself provided a sacrifice

In Abraham's story, there was a substitute sacrifice, but 2,100 years later, there wasn't. Jesus died. We cannot comprehend how God felt as He watched Abraham play out this prophetic scene, knowing that He would watch His one and only Son being nailed to a cross.

Some of us might struggle with the whole concept of sacrifice – even Christians who have been journeying with Jesus a long time. I think it's because a need for justice is hardwired into us. From big things to small things. When I get cut up by others on my commute, for example, everything in me wants to 'seek justice'.

So we all want justice, just perhaps not for ourselves. Have you noticed that? We all mess up; we are all deserving of some kind of judgment and punishment. But God provided a 'lamb' to take all of this on our behalf. For me, the idea of people facing hell as the ultimate justice is a horror story. This whole thing about Jesus is about rescue. Only Christ can satisfy and only Christ can save.

God provided for Abraham and He also provided for us. Often we fall into the trap of talking about God's provision in terms of a new car or holiday. But actually, the first time the term Jehovah Jireh ('God will provide') was used, as we read in Genesis 22, it actually meant ultimate provision. And the ultimate provision was and is Christ. And that's it.

I think that, because of the ultimate sacrifice and provision of Christ, and because of God's extravagant love for us, our lives should be a massive outpouring of thankfulness. We can resist the urge to seek justice over such small things, knowing that, by God's grace, we do not have to fear hell! I also feel we should be among the most generous and sacrificial people on the face of the planet. Opening up our homes, giving freely, lending without expecting back, offering generous words, looking for the good in others, being gracious, forgiving quickly. We've been spared death, after all!

We need God. We need His provision to face what lies ahead in this life. But we also need His ultimate provision of the blood of Jesus, which saves us – and promises us the kingdom of heaven. So let's pray for our hearts to be characterised by thankfulness and joy. Let's pray that we are the most sacrificial and grateful people so that others notice the difference. Let's pray that because we now have the Spirit of God within us, we can reflect God. This is what truly gets my heart pumping! How about you?

'Blessed are the meek,
for they will inherit the earth.'

MATTHEW 5:5

'Refrain from anger
and turn from wrath;
do not fret — it leads only to evil...
But the meek will inherit the land
and enjoy peace and prosperity.'

PSALM 37:8,11

Two

A self-destruct button

It might surprise you that 'Blessed are the meek' is one of my favourite Beatitudes. To be meek (gentle, kind, humble etc) is what I've tried to strive towards over the years. It's taking a lot of work! But I believe it's right at the heart of what God wants for us.

A few years ago, my wife Karen and I moved to a small village in South West England, and found ourselves living next to the world's grumpiest neighbour. I'm sure you haven't got a grumpy neighbour (or indeed *aren't* a grumpy neighbour!) but you can imagine it: whatever we did, he would get snippy and we'd get knocks on the door about anything and everything.

One time, I was out on the road for Christian Vision for Men. I'd been away for three days when Karen phoned me up in tears. Our neighbour had knocked on our door and as soon as Karen opened it, he'd started shouting, spitting and raging in her face. As she tearily explained what had happened, I asked, 'What was it all about, sweetheart?'

I had previously built a little frame – this will probably also surprise you! – for some climbing roses at the back of my garden. It was very nice, actually! It was about the same height as the fence that divided our gardens, but apparently, from our neighbour's point of view, he could see it and he thought I was building an outbuilding. I don't know how he got that impression, it's literally just a trellis, but I could feel the temptation to put him in his place – and the anger started to burn inside. In his rage he had shouted in my wife's face – what was I going to do?

Worst of all, I was miles away and had a full schedule of speaking engagements so I wouldn't be home for at least another two days. During that time, my thoughts often turned to my neighbour. In my mind, I rehearsed what I would say to him. I started to relish the thought of turning up on his doorstep and giving him an eloquent and devastating piece of my mind. I kept hearing the pain, stress and angst in Karen's voice and my anger kept rising to the surface. I love my wife. A lot. She's the most important thing in my world. Don't have a go at my wife – that is my red self-destruct button. Followed very quickly by my kids and then the dog. The cat is further down the hierarchy. But don't have a go at my cat either...

Anyway, when I finally got home, the first thing I did was place my bags in the hallway and, without even taking my jacket off, walk back out of the door, round to my neighbour's to deliver my – by now – finely honed speech.

It was then that the Holy Spirit intercepted me.

I had a choice. I took a deep breath, went back into my house and grabbed a packet of my favourite cakes (fondant fancies, in case you're interested) and went back to my neighbour's. I knocked on his door and he opened it so quickly, I suspect to this day that he'd been waiting for me. He opened his mouth to launch into a tirade, clearly ready for a verbal fight, and I simultaneously held out the packet of cakes. He froze with his mouth open, the shout seemingly stuck in his throat.

'Are you OK?' I asked. 'I've heard we've upset you, so I thought I would pop over to see if you'd like a cup of tea and a cake? I'm very sorry.'

'What?' he said, looking a bit pensive.

'I'm sorry,' I said again.

'Oh. Well, I'm very cross that you're building a huge garage or shed in your back garden.' An assertive look came back into his eyes.

'I'm not, actually. It's a frame for some climbing roses.'

'Oh,' he said again, looking bemused and then down at the floor.

'Would you like a cake?' I said. 'Maybe a cup of tea? Anyway, how are you?'

With that, he burst into tears.

Turns out his wife was in hospital and he was being tested for cancer. Added to this, there was an ongoing feud in his family. He poured his heart out on his doorstep and then we went in and had cake, a cup of tea and a nice chat together.

We never became great mates after that and he never did say sorry to Karen. But we did enjoy a pleasant and civilised, neighbourly relationship from that day on. And as far as I remember, we even got a Christmas card that year.

Looking at those two Bible passages (Matthew 5:5 and Psalm 37:8,11), it seems that Jesus was quoting or possibly linking back to Psalm 37. Anger, wrath, fretting... inevitably leads to evil. But meekness leads to peace and prosperity.

I really believe that if you're a follower of Christ, there is no excuse for losing it. Now I'm not saying we never will, because we're also sinners saved by grace, and we all have our moments. But as children of the living God, we're characterised by gentleness. I believe that we can be full of zeal, driven and passionate (even aggressive when it comes to pushing back against the devil), but I believe we're characterised by calm as well.

We all have a self-destruct button. And that button is pushed by different things for different people. For you, it might be your kids' messy bedrooms, someone at work who gets under your skin, a situation at church... anything. We've all got the potential to lose it. But in those moments we have a choice. We can be people of the opposite spirit. We can respond to anger with love. We can believe the best and give the benefit of the doubt. We can show that the Holy Spirit leads us into a different way of living. Because either the Spirit of God is alive in us, or not. And with Him, we can handle situations distinctly differently to others. Being gentle, kind and humble – meek – is part of following the way of Jesus.

'Blessed are the pure in heart,
for they will see God.'

MATTHEW 5:8

'When someone invites you to a
wedding feast, do not take the place
of honour... take the lowest place...
For all those who exalt themselves
will be humbled, and those who
humble themselves will be exalted.'

LUKE 14:8,10-11

Three

Take your seat

The parable of the guests in Luke 14 is so crucial for us in learning to have a humble and pure heart. Jesus began speaking to the invited guests when He noticed they had been picking out the places of honour at the table. I like this passage. I think it's a very important principle. Never assume that you've 'made it', basically.

I was once invited to speak at a big conference. As often happens with me, I was the keynote speaker but no one really knew who I was! People might have heard my name, but they didn't know what I looked like. Maybe they thought I would be a lot taller in real life – that happens a lot!

Anyway, I went to this conference and eventually got in (I'd lost my ticket) and saw there were loads and loads of plastic flip-down chairs. But at the front I could see this row of very big, comfy, padded chairs. I actually find that a bit embarrassing, if I'm honest. And often after I speak I get an attack of shyness and I like to disappear out the back somewhere and hide. I don't know why, it's weird...

So I decided to sit about halfway back on a plastic chair, when this person recognised me.

'Are you the speaker?' he asked.

'Yeah.'

'Oh, I'm a steward. And a seat has been reserved for you at the front.'

'I'm quite happy here.'

'You need to at least see the tech person.'

'OK, I'll do that.' I could see the tech guy at the back.

'But you've got to go down the front.'

'Oh no, I'm quite happy here. I'll come down during the song before I go up.'

'OK,' the steward said defeatedly before walking away.

So I went to sort out the tech stuff, sat back down in my

plastic chair, and the steward came back.

'Um, sorry, if you don't come and move down I'm going to get told off for not doing my job.'

'You're kidding me?'

'No, you've really got to go and move down to the front.'

So, for not wanting someone to get told off, I obediently went down to the front. And as I approached the front rows, this security guard stopped me.

'This is for the speakers, and the host of the conference.'

'Oh, sorry, mate, I am a speaker.'

'Who are you?'

'Carl Beech.'

'Who's Carl Beech?'

'...I think I'm on the programme. I'm doing the main talk tonight.'

At that he gasped and said, 'Don't tell the organisers I stopped you!'

I thought to myself, 'What kind of a gig is this?'

As I went to sit down, there was actually a seat labelled 'Pastor Carl Beech'. (I've never been called that before – everyone calls me 'Beechy'!) So I felt excruciatingly embarrassed. But at the end of the day, it was great because I preached and people got saved! (Then I disappeared out the back and found a coffee shop.)

Point being, I'd rather it was that way around. It would have been worse if I'd tried to go down and security stopped me and actually I wasn't meant to be down the front. Imagine how embarrassing that would have been! But there's got to be a balance. We honour people, we respect people, but no one is more important than anyone else in the eyes of God.

Nowadays, one of my absolutely key principles when I speak at conferences and festivals is that I stay or camp where the festival-goers stay. I hang out in the main areas. I queue with everyone else for food and drinks. I use the same showers and toilets. It doesn't sound like much, but it's my way of keeping pride at bay.

Worrying about our position and status is natural, yet something we have to curb when following the way. I had once been leading a large, multi-congregational Baptist Church when I moved on to serve another leader as his 'number two' on the team. Many people at the time thought I was mad. They would ask: 'Why on earth would you leave senior leadership to work for someone else again?'

Leadership has many privileges. You are the culture setter. You can make final decisions and you are, in a sense, the master of your own destiny. It has its pressures, but the sense of freedom is a fantastic thing. However, you also get your ego stroked. You walk into a room and people take notice of what you have to say. You get announced as 'the leader'. You get a seat at the table of some key meetings. It's fun, but if you're not careful, it can play havoc with your heart.

There is no doubt that God uses profile, personality and leadership. You see that all the way through the Bible. But it beholds leaders to hear God's call and not let ego or vanity get in the way of taking what could be viewed as a 'step back' (in human terms) in order to get the work of the kingdom done. I suspect that when we die and meet Jesus, the status or position we had in the eyes of men and women will count for very, very little indeed!

So much of what we read in Matthew 5–7 is about the heart and character – the result of refinement by the Holy Spirit. But so much also comes from actually making a conscious decision to be a certain way, or respond in a certain way. The way to train your heart to be humble is to actually *do* humble things. Simple! Practise humility. Serve other people, tidy stuff up when you see it and don't assume your car should be parked in a certain place. No matter what position you find yourself in, do humble things. Maybe you could apologise to your kids or be more gracious? Maybe you could own up to something you let slip at work?

Another thing I like to do is always be on the lookout for people I can look up to. Perhaps there is someone who I see as wise, or full of peace. I might even be their boss, but I look to them to lead me in these things. In this way I submit to God in my heart, knowing that I have in no way 'made it' – whatever that really means.

I want to have a pure and humble heart, and I know that the whole thing is about loving God and loving people. If pride is getting in the way of me doing this, I need to root it out.

So, let me ask you, what seat are you going to take at work, at home, at church, this week?

'Blessed are the peacemakers,
for they will be called
children of God.'

MATTHEW 5:9

Four

Holidays in Syria
— Linda McKay

I'd like to do something a little different now and share the testimony of Linda McKay. She poured out her life to bring the peace of Christ into some of the most heart-breaking, dangerous and desperate places around the world. And all because of her love for Jesus. Linda says she learned to do this from a very early age, growing up as a pastor's kid...

I was born in 1983 in South Africa, a country in the grip of apartheid. My parents had moved out there to find wealth, and they did – but they found it in the form of Jesus. Shortly after my first birthday we returned to the UK, and when I was five, I gave my life to Jesus. When I look back now I can see how, even from that age, God's hand was on me, preparing me for the adventures to come in taking His peace into other people's lives.

I always felt drawn to go back to the nation of my birth. I studied languages at university, followed by a master's degree in Intercultural Communication. It was this that took me back to South Africa. I couldn't just write a dissertation on how best to help a certain township, I needed to stay there and put it into action. So for three years I called that township home, a place where I was told I was at risk of being murdered, just for being white. I lived right in the midst of the poverty and turmoil, with little water or electricity. Death was a part of everyday life. It had some of the highest infection rates of HIV/AIDS in the world – around 40% of the population. My neighbours, by age 11, knew how to dig graves. I found myself burying some of the teenagers I lived and worked with in unmarked dirt graves. It was one of the hardest things I have ever had to do.

In such conditions you learn quickly how important it is to know – *really* know – who Jesus is and what He has done. With that knowledge, peace doesn't have to be circumstantial and the most desperate places on earth can still be full of joy and hope. Through many tears I learned that being present with people in the midst of intense pain was both all I could do, and the best I could do.

During my time there, we developed a children's village for orphaned children, built nursery schools and set up feeding schemes and small business enterprises. But still, Jesus was the truest peace and purest hope I could offer.

When I came back to the UK I began leading a missions team across Europe. We came alongside churches, encouraging them to get out and interact with their communities. My favourite places to visit were the ones I was told were 'too hard' (or 'dark') and that what we did 'wouldn't work there'. When I heard that, I knew they just hadn't yet met the Jesus I knew.

It was for this reason that I was prompted to go to France. One afternoon we had no translator, so we took a guitar and worshipped in front of a town hall. Within the space of 45 minutes we had person after person approach us, some prompted to join in with the worship, and some being physically healed as they did so. But my favourite encounter was with a young gypsy girl, who must have been no older than eight. She had been sent to beg money from us by her mum, who we could see on the other side of the square. By the time she reached us she had tears rolling down her cheeks and she uttered, 'I need God. Pray for me.' It's not our words or deeds that transform lives – it's simply carrying God's presence into places of darkness.

A few years and a fair few countries later, I got to head up a team working with refugees in the Jordanian town of Mafraq on the Syrian border. The Syrian civil war was rife, and there were thousands of refugees arriving every week in this poor, desert town. We had no knowledge of the culture or the language, but we knew the God of hope.

At the time, all we could do was visit the homes of our Syrian neighbours, drink tea and learn Arabic as we went. We could hear bombs being dropped across the border – there was one night when a drone was shot out of the air less than a mile away. We knew there was a jihadist militant group in town, so we had to be very careful with what we did and said. There was definitely opportunity to be fearful, but I honestly cannot remember feeling scared. I am convinced that was because I knew that my peace wasn't dependent on the circumstances.

I believe there is a real link between hope and peace. So much of our strategy in Jordan was to bring hope into lives, families and situations. We would take coach-loads of children on trips to the zoo, and we once threw a birthday party for 160 kids in the middle of the desert because none of them had celebrated a birthday since the war broke out. As we got to know the community, we set up a kids club in the centre of the village, and ended up with about 200 coming every week. We combined trauma therapy with playing, and simply gave them the opportunity to be kids in the midst of the chaos. For many of the onlooking parents, it was the first smiles they'd seen from their children in days, weeks or even months.

There was one family we worked with, which included a five-year-old girl who was probably the most traumatised child I'd ever met. If she saw the colour red, she would have incredible panic attacks because she'd seen so much blood. Seeing people being murdered on the streets was normal for her. One bitterly cold evening, we visited the family before her older sister was due in for an operation. Her mum was also suffering badly from bomb shrapnel wounds in her leg. There was so much fear and hopelessness, but we knew we could bring Jesus into the midst of it. We took a guitar and sat and worshipped with them. The young girl got up and started dancing. Both her parents, transfixed by the sight, threw off their blankets and started weeping. The cold didn't matter anymore. It was apparent that they'd never seen their daughter dance before. It didn't change their situation, but in that moment, peace came into their lives.

We went on to see many in the community come to know Jesus. You couldn't preach Jesus, but you could 'show' Him. One man told me of a dream in which he saw someone dressed as a prince coming towards him on a horse, carrying a double-edged sword. He said he instantly knew this man was the Prince of peace. In situations like that, all we had to do was open our Bibles and show them who Jesus was, and they would devour the truth for themselves.

Towards the end of my time in Jordan, I felt God calling me back to England. I am now a chaplain for people who have left prison or rehab and want to learn what it really means to live for Jesus. I had never worked with ex-offenders or those in recovery from life-controlling addictions before. The challenges may be new, but my strategy is still simply to be present in the midst of the chaos; bringing with me the peace I have in Jesus.

I could not be prouder watching these people grow. The life I see them now living has not been their 'normal'.

I know their stories, and so when I see their smiles and hear their laughter, when I take them along to a ballroom dance lesson or drop them off at their first day of work, I want to pause the moment and savour it for a while. Those are the moments that the watching world does not recognise as miracles. But it's then that I truly see peace beyond comprehension.

I'll conclude my stories of God's peace with one particularly memorable moment. It was one that utterly convinced me that God is not fazed by the storms around us, no matter how great they may seem. On a trip to Rwanda, I was driven for hours through the bush to speak at a conference. It was in a remote village and the church was only partially built, so the ladies moved around the hut throughout the day to follow the shade. I was sharing with them that children are often afraid of storms, until they learn by watching their parents that they don't need to be scared – and that I believe we can do the same with God. As I finished talking, an actual storm started rolling in from the surrounding hills. As the rain picked up, everyone huddled under the part of the church that had a roof. Then, with a huge noise, a bolt of lightning came through the hole in the roof and struck the ground between the first row and where I was sitting. I have never felt power like it. But the fear that could have been present was dispelled by laughter at knowing who was in control.

I love how far God will go to show us that He knows. It doesn't matter what storm you're in, it doesn't have to rob you of the peace in your life. And that is the truth we can take with us. Focusing on God's face and not the storm will bring peace – and it's a peace that can be passed on.

'Blessed are you when people insult you, persecute you and falsely say all kinds of evil against you because of me. Rejoice and be glad, because great is your reward in heaven'

MATTHEW 5:11–12

'The disciples went and woke [Jesus]... He got up and rebuked the wind and the raging waters; the storm subsided, and all was calm.'

LUKE 8:24

Five

Smile
at the storm

Have you ever found yourself wanting to write a really stinging text message, email or letter to someone in defence of yourself? Or is it just me? Have you ever faced a situation where there's been an unjust accusation made against you, and in your mind you craft an amazingly shrewd and venomous response back? One that would take that person or people down!

Have you ever done that? I've written or thought of some amazing retaliations in my time! But I'm glad for the times I didn't say or send them. It's the worst thing you could do with an email – actually send it – isn't it?

If you've ever been in leadership, you might have started off under the mistaken impression that everyone would always love you and know that you do everything for the Lord and His people. That normally lasts about ten days before things start to go a bit pear-shaped. And unfortunately, over the years, I have been in a number of meetings where I've faced some really tough stuff.

I remember as a senior leader, many years ago, being summoned to a meeting by my fellow leaders. I mean, this was a big church; there was a lot going on. A lot to handle. And one Sunday night, ironically after a Communion service, one of the elders said, 'We need you to come to a meeting tomorrow evening.'

I said, 'Oh, that doesn't sound good, what is it?'

'We'll tell you when you get there.'

So, really bad then.

Anyway, as it turned out, I turned up at this meeting to be greeted by a room full of people all sitting on chairs in a circle. The only seat left was this little footstool. So I sat down (seriously, this is the actual truth) and everyone was towering high above me. So I, the senior pastor, was like a child in the corner, with no clue as to what was going on.

This is how you learn humility; the Lord has a plan.

Then it got worse. Someone in the circle had a clipboard with a long list of allegations against me. They were read out systematically in front of everyone.

After allegation number one, I was like: 'I think I might have said that but that sounds a bit twisted.'

Allegation two: 'I don't think I've ever *been* to that place.'

Allegation three: 'That is definitely not me!'

Anyway, by allegation four I sat there thinking, 'I'm going to go DEFCON 1 here. I'm going to make everyone realise that I am the senior pastor, the "anointed one", and I am going to call down the fire of heaven and burn up the entire eldership!' My heart had claws around it and I could feel the anger – the venom – surfacing.

And then I felt the voice of the Spirit whispering in my ear. As I'd gone out the door of our house earlier that evening, Karen had said to me, 'I've got a feeling this is going to be a bad meeting.'

'I think you might be right,' I said.

'I've got a little song that I sing.'

'Have you?'

'Yes. I used to sing it in Sunday school.'

'OK, what is it?'

And I can't remember the rhythm but she said, 'It's: "With Jesus in the vessel you can smile at the storm..."'

So there I'm sitting, on my little footstool, and in my head I'm going, 'With Jesus in the vessel you can smile at the storm.' And above the voice of the person reading out the allegations, which I'd stopped listening to, another said, 'Why are you smiling?'

'I've just got the peace of the Lord.'

'Why is that?'

'Well, I don't think any of this is true really.'

Then another leader said, 'To be honest, I've sat here

and I've listened, and all of this is absolutely ridiculous. I can't believe we called this meeting.' (I thought they could have piped up at allegation two!)

Everyone stood up from their normal chairs and me from my stool. The person who'd accused me looked crestfallen and said, 'I need to fall on my sword and resign!'

'We're not in *Seven Samurai*,' I said, 'We're brothers. It's OK.'

It takes courage for people to say sorry, and for others to forgive, in these sorts of situations. Being falsely accused can hurt deeply. But forgiveness and grace are part of who we are as kingdom people. We are called to a higher way.

So, in the end we smoothed things out and planned a dinner together as families. And in my head I still had the words: 'With Jesus in the vessel you can smile at the storm.'

False accusations made against us may go even further than my experience that Monday evening. Those allegations were dropped, after all. So, what if we face a situation that is even more unbearable and unjust?

Well, Jesus role-modelled it, didn't He? When He was facing accusations, every single one of them false and leading to death on a cross, He stayed silent (Matthew 26:63). We know the rest of the story. We know that Jesus knew He had to die so that He could rise again and give humankind a way to God. Now He is in His rightful place in heaven, at the right hand of God (Mark 16:19). That is why I believe Matthew 5 when it says 'great is your reward in heaven' (v11). That is why we can smile at the storm today. We have Jesus, the one who can and will command the storm to pass.

If I could pass on one tip to help you when you face accusations or a sense of injustice, it's this: simply give it to heaven and let heaven decide. Pray for peace and trust that God will deal with it. I've made the conscious choice to do this many times over the years and I've always known peace as a result.

'You are the salt of the earth.
But if the salt loses its saltiness,
how can it be made salty again?
It is no longer good for anything,
except to be thrown out and
trampled underfoot. You are the light
of the world. A town built on a hill
cannot be hidden... In the same way,
let your light shine before others,
that they may see your good deeds
and glorify your Father in heaven.'

MATTHEW 5:13-14,16

Six

Salt

I remember my first proper job working in a bank. We had this big sales campaign that happened to be based around astrology symbols. (Bit awkward for a follower of Jesus, you might say.) In the retail part of the bank, they had this pyramid. When you opened a door in the pyramid, it would say something like, 'Sagittarius – You need to invest in a pension.' Or, 'Pisces – You need to look at unit trusts.' So they developed this whole thing around astrology.

At the time, I was in my early twenties, and had managed to become one of the top salesmen in London. So the managers asked me to do some retail training, and they got everyone – all the sales staff – in the boardroom together.

That morning, I went over to the regional sales director, and said that I couldn't do it.

'Why is that?' he asked.

'Because it's all astrology stuff.'

'It's all rubbish, isn't it? It's just a marketing thing.'

'Yeah, I know, but I'm a Christian.'

'Yeah, I'm C of E, so what?'

'No, I follow Jesus, and it's not compatible with what I believe. I can't do the training.'

So I didn't go.

Afterwards, this director literally had my back against the wall. He screamed and shouted that I could forget about ever being promoted, that I was finished, that as long as he worked at that bank, I was stuffed.

I'd just got married and had a mortgage to pay. I went home that day thinking my world had fallen apart. But I knew that I could trust in God. I asked a few people at church to pray, and spoke to a couple of retired bank managers. They praised me for standing my ground, but I'll admit it didn't make me feel any better about my career.

About a month later, we were all called into a staff meeting, and that same regional sales director announced that the bank was changing. There was going to be a swathe of redundancies, and the first person being made redundant was him. He left a week later.

Then I got called into a meeting. I thought it was the end for me too. But instead they told me I was going to be promoted.

I believe God was teaching me something. This story is just a small example of what it might mean to keep our 'saltiness' at all costs. Would I have preferred to keep my job over compromising my faith? Would I have preferred security over shining a light for God? Humanly speaking, yes, probably! In my natural mind, my needs come first. But God calls us to more than that. Very graciously, God blessed me in this situation. But at the time I had to trust Him to work it all out.

As we follow Jesus today, there will be many occasions when we'll have to choose between either hiding who we are, or staying faithful to what we believe. Jesus' teaching in Matthew 5 is so opposite to the way of the world. So we can live, behave, talk, and do the things that ultimately point others to Jesus. It may cost us, but we can trust that God will always be with us.

When I look at the world we are trying to reach it can be heart-breaking. You look at the stats on self-harming, suicide, depression, gender confusion, addiction... and you wonder where we can even start. As followers of Christ we need to do all we can to shine light into darkness and make Jesus known, because the truth is that only He can satisfy.

Perhaps the need for followers of the way to be salt and light is more urgent now than ever before. In Jesus' time, salt was rubbed into meat to stop it from rotting

– to hinder the decaying process. And that's our call. Wherever you are, whatever you do, stop the rot and shine the light of Christ.

'if you are offering your gift at the altar and there remember that your brother or sister has something against you... go and be reconciled to them: then come and offer your gift.'

MATTHEW 5:23-24

'Be devoted to one another in love. Honour one another above yourselves. Never be lacking in zeal, but keep your spiritual fervour, serving the Lord... Share with the Lord's people who are in need. Practise hospitality.'

ROMANS 12:10-11,13

Seven

Dinner's ready

What would it look like if we honoured others above ourselves? How would it change the way we behave, the way we talk and serve, and the things we do?

When Karen and I were first going out, she cooked me dinner at her mum's house. Unbeknownst to Karen, her mum had left oven cleaner in the oven. The meal ended up in the bin and I decided that it'd be a good idea to mock her about it. Years later, I was cooking dinner when the memory of this came flooding back. (Isn't it weird when that happens?) No one had mentioned it, nothing had been said about it, but I remembered it. So I went into the lounge where Karen was sitting, and said, 'Do you remember that time at your mum's when dinner was ruined and I made fun of you? Did I upset you?'

She thought about it for a second and then said, 'You did actually, and it knocked my confidence for a while.'

'Oh. Would you forgive me? I'm sorry.'

'Of course I do... just don't do it again!'

As I left to get back to cooking, I noticed she had a tear in her eye. I guess I really had hurt her all those years ago, and I think it was the Holy Spirit bringing it back to me. It's a little tiny thing, isn't it? But I'd upset my wife and I'm glad we'd resolved it.

Something I've realised about honouring others is that just saying sorry for hurting them is not really enough. But by asking for forgiveness, we give the person a choice – we place the power in their hands. It creates a completely different vibe. You've got an undefended heart and you're prepared for them to say, 'Actually you did hurt me.' And reconciliation can take place. I think this is part of what it means to lay our lives down to honour one another.

When it comes to mutual submission and honour in my marriage, I like to think I'm the thorn on the rose – that I'll take the muck, so that my wife can have a beautiful life. But I know that she wants to do the same for me. Imagine if we were all walking around trying to be the thorns on the rose – all being prepared to lay our lives down for one another. All using our words to honour rather than slam or shame.

When we honour and submit to each other we are following the way. It's what Jesus did – He literally laid down His life for us. We're also mirroring the Trinity. The Spirit honoured Jesus when He descended on Him like a dove at His baptism. Jesus submitted to the Father's will by going to the cross. The Father placed Jesus at His right hand in heaven – the highest honour.

Let's think about the way we talk *with* one another, and the way we talk *about* one another. If you are a follower of the way, then you are a culture setter wherever you are. Gossiping, joking at the expense of another, placing blame – it all carries massive impact and weight. Mutual submission is apologising first, speaking kind words, and being patient with one another. So whether it's through cooking a meal – or refraining from making a mockery of someone's failed attempt to cook a meal – let us submit to and honour those around us. If we do so, I'll tell you what it will look like: it will look like Jesus.

'You have heard that it was said, "Eye for eye, and tooth for tooth." But I tell you, do not resist an evil person. If anyone slaps you on the right cheek, turn to them the other cheek also. And if anyone wants to sue you and take your shirt, hand over your coat as well. If anyone forces you to go one mile, go with them two miles. Give to the one who asks you, and do not turn away from the one who wants to borrow from you.'

MATTHEW 5:38-42

Eight

Putting stones in shoes

A few years ago, for a brief period of time, I had a sports car. It was a very splendid Toyota GT86, and I loved it. Now I knew that I wouldn't have it for long, so I used it as much as possible.

And then I crashed it.

At 5mph.

Yes, you read that right, I was going a mere 5mph.

Let me explain.

It was December, and I was about a quarter of a mile from my house. It was dark, it was raining, I was in a queue of traffic, and I was looking out of the window. The wrong window. In fact, I was looking out of the side window when I should've been looking at the traffic in front. And then the inevitable happened. The car in front of me moved off, I pulled away as well, then that car stalled and I rolled gently into the back of it.

This was a very low speed accident and really shouldn't have caused much damage. However, the car I rolled into was a 1989 Vauxhall Nova, which is built like a tank with a rubber bumper the size of Wales. My GT86 was low-slung and the front bumper was built predominantly from plastic. It ever so gently nudged underneath the bumper of the Vauxhall Nova.

Of course, I immediately got out of my car, walked to the car in front, tapped on the window and said, 'I'm terribly sorry... Merry Christmas!' with a sheepish smile on my face.

'Why did you do that?' she said (the driver being a young lady).

'Honestly, because I wasn't looking.'

'Well, shall we look at the damage?'

'That's a good idea,' I said, and we both walked around to the back of her car together.

It was a sight for sore eyes. Her car was pretty badly beaten up anyway – in all honesty, it was probably only worth about £200.

'I don't think my car has any damage,' she decided. 'You've not been so lucky, though, have you?'

It was fair to say that she was right. There was no visible damage to her car, but mine had turned into a pterodactyl. You see, the GT86 had a high-tech feature called a crumple zone, designed to absorb some of the force of a head-on collision. However, it seemed that on this occasion it had somewhat over-performed. Pretty much the entire front end of my car had folded up into a twisted, pointed sculpture that looked like this particular type of dinosaur. An absolute nightmare.

Anyway, because there wasn't any damage to her car, and we happily swapped numbers just in case, that was that.

About a week went by and I hadn't heard anything from the young driver of the old Vauxhall Nova. And then I got a text message, which went something like this: 'I had my car professionally assessed by a mechanic, and it seems there is over £500 worth of damage to my car. But if you send me a cheque for £100, we can forget all about it.'

I was furious. I mean, I'm from Romford, Essex, so I know a scam. I know when I'm being ripped off. It was absolutely ridiculous. The car was an old wreck – it wasn't even worth £500!

But then, there's this little thing called living with an opposite spirit. I knew I had to get a grip on my heart. So I metaphorically put myself in the corner and gave myself a very strong talking to. I sent her a text back saying that I could come down and drop off some money. Only, I didn't write the cheque for £100, I wrote it for £150. I drove to her house (it was easy to find, because I saw her undamaged car on the driveway) and knocked on the door. When she answered, I said, 'Here is the cheque you've asked for, but I added a little extra by way of an apology. Sorry again for inconveniencing you. I just want to bless you.'

'What do you mean, "bless me"?'

'Well, it's just the way I want to live my life.'

'What?'

'Well, actually, I'm one of those Christian types of people.'

'A Christian?'

'Yes,' I said, 'and I'm sorry I crashed into you.'

'Bless me?'

'Yes. Anyway, here's the cheque. It's only an extra 50 quid, but I hope it's useful with a car to repair coming up to Christmas.'

She looked at me blankly for a moment. And then she went a bit pale when she looked down at the cheque and saw it was from 'Reverend Carl Beech'.

I'll be honest with you, part of me wanted to say something like: 'And if you steal from a man of God you could be struck down by lightning – many bad things could befall you and your family!' But of course, I didn't. Instead, I smiled sweetly, turned on my heel, strode back past her undamaged car to my pterodactyl and drove away.

Inside, I was thinking that she probably wouldn't cash the cheque. I was thinking that she would be so overcome by grace and the love of Christ that she would never be able to pay the cheque in. Going by my bank statement, I was wrong. She paid in the cheque later that afternoon. But here's the thing, it was worth the risk.

Once again, let me explain.

Let's imagine that I had stood my ground and refused to give her the money; instead, arguing and pointing out the error of her thieving ways. Let's then imagine that a year or two later she encounters you, and you invite her to an Alpha course. But she turns to you and says, 'I met this Christian once. Turns out he was a total pig, a really aggressive guy,' etc. Well, that would really ship your evangelism, wouldn't it?

Alternatively, you might meet her one day and invite her to the Alpha course – and she remembers this crazy guy who confounded her. I think she's much more likely to respond to the gospel because I did something crazy like give her a few extra quid. As I said, it was worth the risk.

I like to think I 'put a stone in her shoe'. I think she now has a permanent gospel limp. She will be wondering what on earth I was all about. I mean, who does stuff like that? I'll tell you who does stuff like that – we do! We are the people who live with an opposite spirit. Jesus said, when someone forces you to go a mile, go an extra mile. When someone wants the shirt off your back, give them your coat as well.

It strikes me that we have daily opportunities to react to situations in a radically different way to most people. But here's the thing: to live this way is extremely tough. It seemingly goes against every instinct. Everything in us wants justice (well, our idea of justice) in these sorts of situations. Everything in us wants the truth to be known. We want people to recognise the folly and error of their ways. We can't bear the fact that someone is walking around having got the upper hand over us. We don't like to think we've looked weak – like a thin, cheap doormat stamped into the ground. But that's because we have lost sight of the bigger picture.

My Bible tells me that God made the heavens and the earth. It tells me that He made us. It tells me that He knows every hair on our heads, every word on our tongues, and every day of our lives. It also tells me that He loves us, and that we exist because of His grace. Nanosecond by nanosecond, He sustains us. Should God want to shut the whole show down, He could. It is only because of His grace that you can read this, have an opinion, and have the freedom to choose how to act in any given situation. He has asked us to live and act with grace.

When we realise just how blessed we all are to even draw a breath, then it really puts in perspective how silly it is when we get the hump over such minor stuff. To take the higher path (which is also a very narrow path, according to Jesus' teaching in Matthew 7), is to overlook an insult, accept a small, personal injustice, give someone the benefit of the doubt, refuse to bicker on social media, let someone take our place in the line – even speak well of those who have antagonised us and made our lives difficult.

I can guess what you're thinking: this is mad, and a great way to become a professional doormat! You may be right, but I would rather save my emotional energy for a fight that really matters. Frankly, parking spaces, someone pulling a fast one, someone getting more recognition than me, or a rude and factually incorrect email... these things just don't seem that important when you consider how much grace God has shown us.

Besides... putting stones in people's shoes is actually quite a lot of fun.

'If you love those who love you,
what reward will you get?
Are not even the tax collectors doing
that? And if you greet only
your own people, what are you doing
more than others?
Do not even pagans do that?
Be perfect, therefore,
as your heavenly Father is perfect.'

MATTHEW 5:46-48

Nine

Start loving people

Karen and I recently got involved with a scheme through which we've befriended an elderly gentleman in his eighties (let's call him Richard). He can't see very well, and lives alone. So he comes round to our place for dinner from time to time, and Karen takes him to the supermarket to do the shopping and all that kind of stuff. It's great.

But I tell you something – doing that can be quite difficult. Richard can be a bit blunt and grumpy. Sometimes, when I've had a long week, the last thing I want is someone coming round to my house, when all they want to do is moan. But weirdly I've grown really attached to him. It's true! And I know that Karen has too – she's always worrying about him and wondering how he is.

I've come to learn that the more you serve people, even someone you'd rather not serve, the more your feelings and attitude change towards them. It's easy to love those we get on with, are related to or just find lovable, isn't it? But as followers of the way, we're called to more than that.

I've found that the more you love and serve someone, no matter who they are, the more you start to actually love them. It's really very strange. We've never had anything back from Richard, and he can still be as grumpy as ever, yet Karen and I are incredibly fond of him.

I believe it's because God starts working in our hearts when we step out in obedience to Him. The more we give out to other people, the more joy God gives to us. The more you lay your life down, the more life you receive. It's all part of God's topsy-turvy, upside-down kingdom!

When we feel down, disappointed or grumbly ourselves, the temptation is to retreat inwards and nurse our wounds. But I know the cure is to just start loving people. You won't feel like it at first, but trust me, it's God's way.

Just start loving people. Start getting involved in

schemes or church groups. Lay your life down. You might actually discover what joy is – real joy. And after all, we have the most perfect role model, don't we? Jesus loved us, each and every one of us, even when we were totally unlovable. He laid His life down. If we ever feel we've got the right to have the hump, and take it out on people, let's remember that Jesus truly had the right, but He chose to forgive even those who nailed Him to a cross. That's our example to follow!

'when you pray, go into your room,
close the door and pray to your
Father, who is unseen.
Then your Father, who sees what
is done in secret, will reward you.
And when you pray, do not keep on
babbling like pagans, for they think
they will be heard because of their
many words. Do not be like them,
for your Father knows
what you need before you ask him.'

MATTHEW 6:6-8

Ten

A tree in the sun

For the last ten years or so, I've been taking groups to a sports resort in Lanzarote. Basically, you go there to eat good food, drink ice-cold drinks in perpetually beautiful weather (it's not far off the coast of West Africa) and absolutely hammer your body in long, mountainous cycle rides, high intensity gym workouts, running, swimming and anything else that the resort can think of to inflict pain.

There is a signature bicycle climb called 'Tabyesco' (not Tabasco – the sauce isn't nearly as painful). It's a 2,000 feet climb up a valley from the coast, via a succession of hairpin bends. It's tough, always hot, steep and a proper test of cycle fitness. More than that, you have to do some serious miles before you even get to the climb, so your legs are already tired. Grit and determination are definitely required.

One time, on getting to the top, I saw a small tree casting a bit of shadow. It's so exposed on the climb that you basically cook, so this tiny tree was a hugely welcome sight. I got off my bike, grabbed a water bottle and sat on a dusty bit of rock in its shade. Bliss. I can remember feeling a sense of total contentment wash all over me. It was hot. I was tired. But I had water and a bit of shade. I can vividly remember thinking I had everything I needed.

Back in the rat race of friendships, bills to pay, being a dad, husband, charity leader etc, it tends to take a lot more for me to feel content. I want a curry takeaway, Sky TV, an Xbox, gym membership, hobbies, the latest gadget... You know the score.

I'm not appealing to go back to some kind of over-the-top simplicity but it's food for thought, isn't it? I have often felt that the Beatitudes and other teaching in the Sermon on the Mount have an underlying call to a simplified life. It all has a beautiful and simple purity about it, and I suspect that the more we live it out, the more our lives will reflect that simplicity.

I don't know about you, but I have very few moments where I can actually just take a breath, talk with God and rest in Him. And those moments are so valuable because I get to think about the things that He wants me to do, and the things He wants for my family. When you rest in the Lord you get perspective, you get wisdom, and you'll think about your recent choices and actions and how you're responding to what life's throwing at you. When that horrible email comes in, when someone presses your self-destruct button, if you've taken time to be in the presence of God, your responses will be different.

So let's ask ourselves: have our lives become too complex for our own good? And if the answer is yes, maybe we ought to take some time out to recover moments of stillness and simple contentment, like the shade of a tree on a blisteringly hot day. I have this suspicion that we would become even more fervent followers of the way for it.

Jesus would often withdraw to quiet places. Have you ever wondered why?

'For if you forgive other people when they sin against you, your heavenly Father will also forgive you. But if you do not forgive others their sins, your Father will not forgive your sins.'

MATTHEW 6:14-15

Eleven

Grace

One of my mates sent me a cool video the other day. I often get sent links to YouTube videos. You might know the kind of thing: base jumpers skimming the ground as they glide through the air at 130mph, ski jumpers crashing, forklift truck drivers going out of control, movie trailers etc. This one was a bit different, though. It was called, 'The thing that eats everything'...

It has to be one of the most mesmerising videos I've ever seen. Everyone I've shown it to has been totally hooked, saying things like, 'I could watch this all day.'

Now, before you think it's an oversized piranha eating a cow, let me explain in more detail. The 'thing that eats everything' is a huge industrial shredding machine, the likes of which you will not have seen before.

The video, minus any commentary, simply consists of a camera pointing into the jaws of the shredder as people tip things into it. A huge industrial-sized fridge gets eaten in seconds. A sofa disappears before your eyes. A huge construction-machine tyre, made from rubber as thick as the Earth's crust, is no contest either. It gets eaten up like paper. At least half of the people I've shown the video to have also shuddered while watching it. I suspect they were thinking what I did: 'I hope no one ever falls into that... that would hurt!'

Watching those massive metal grinding wheels destroy stuff is immensely satisfying. I've tried to think why that is. Is it the engineering? The statistics are indeed impressive, so for all you collectors of data out there, check this out: the world's largest shredder can eat 450 cars an hour. It has a 40 tonne electric, water-cooled motor and the motor end drive takes forces of up to 116 tonnes. If that doesn't mean much to you, let's just say that it is very powerful indeed!

I don't think it's that, though. I think it's something about watching stuff disappear, never to be seen again. Shredded and destroyed for all time. I've watched other giant shredder videos since. An old Volkswagen Beetle. Gone. A van. Gone. An industrial cooker. Gone.

I think we all need an industrial shredder – for life stuff, though, not old sofas. When you first give your life to Jesus Christ, you simultaneously also encounter a shredding machine for all the old rubbish that's hanging around in your life. All the old wrongs, mess, pain and stuff that has generally just hurt you and others. It's a beautiful moment when you first feel truly clean, light and free.

Why is this important for following the teachings of the way of Jesus Christ? Well, put simply, once we have truly experienced the cleansing power of repentance and the remarkable, extravagant grace of Jesus then, perhaps for the first time, we can start to view people through a filter of compassion, patience and forgiveness. Even those we previously found irritating or hurtful to be around. We are all God's children, all trying to navigate our way through the ups and downs of this adventure of life. We all accumulate hurts that can affect the way we interact with others. But when we ourselves experience grace, who are we not to treat others with that same grace?

It often astonishes me when I look at the level of fighting in churches, between brothers and sisters in Christ, especially on social media. Let's model something different to a world that desperately needs to hear, see and experience the power of peace and reconciliation that only Christ can give us.

So, let's try this. Take all that stuff that's lying around in your life that you wish would just go away, give it over to Jesus and experience His forgiveness. And then, in response to His love, forgive others and crucially, yourself. Shred up the past into oblivion.

'Therefore I tell you,
do not worry about your life,
what you will eat or drink; or about
your body, what you will wear.
Is not life more than food,
and the body more than clothes?
Look at the birds of the air;
they do not sow or reap or store
away in barns, and yet your
heavenly Father feeds them.
Are you not much more
valuable than they?'

MATTHEW 6:25-26

Twelve

The Eagle Nebula

One of the key facets of following the way is to be a peacemaker. (We heard Linda's testimony in Chapter Five, which I hope you found really inspiring in this area.) But I've come to realise that if I'm truly to be a peacemaker, I need to be at peace myself, in a very deep and profound way.

When I first planted a church in 1996, I was worried about everything. And when some things did go wrong, I was not prepared for the toll it would take on my then fragile and insecure mindset. I was not a man at peace to start with, and 18 months in, my judgment started to get affected and my perspective was shot to pieces. I was paranoid and stressed. I read far too much into every little nuance of people's words and behaviour. I started to try to control everything in a vain attempt to keep the show on the road. It was then that I realised I couldn't be a peacemaker, bringing the radical message of Jesus' love, when I was in so much conflict myself. Yet I didn't know how to get out of it.

At one point during this period of my life, I found myself leaning against the rubbish skips round the back of the community centre where we used to meet as a church. I couldn't face going into the meeting that should have already started because I felt so insecure and stressed. I knew people didn't like me, and to be honest, I didn't really like myself that much either. It was at that moment that I felt the Spirit of God whisper into my soul in such an acute way, it was game-changing. The conversation went something like this...

'I don't think anybody likes me,' I said.

'Not many people do.'

My heart sank. Could this really be God's voice speaking to me?

'And I'm such a rubbish pastor. I try to help people but it's just not working.'

'Yes, it's not been that good.'

'I don't think I'm being a good husband either because I'm so stressed.'

'Yes, things aren't that great at home, are they?'

'I've spent all my money – and if this doesn't work out, I'm out of ministry already and I've barely started.'

'Yes, you may be out of ministry. That could happen.'

As you can imagine, I was feeling absolutely on the floor. Then, in the midst of this terrible moment, the inner voice whispered something that penetrated my soul.

'You are my son, and I love you, so what's the problem?'

In an instant I felt an incredible peace wash over me. I reached into my rucksack, pulled out my Bible and looked at the concordance in the back. I looked up the word 'son' and it took me to Romans 8:15: 'the Spirit you received brought about your adoption to sonship. And by him we cry, "*Abba*, Father."'

It's hard to explain how electrifying this moment was for me. I knew something profound and significant had happened when I walked into the hall to see only a handful of people, and yet the burden to perform – to please everyone – had lifted off me completely. It was a realisation that if God loved me, nothing else mattered.

When I had first given my life to Jesus from a completely unchurched background, and was facing a lot of opposition from friends, I did something I would never recommend you do in case it goes horribly wrong! I sat on the edge of my bed, not having a clue how to read the Bible, closed my eyes, asked God to speak to me and opened my Bible up.

The verse leapt out at me: 'Never will I leave you; never will I forsake you' (Hebrews 13:5). And I thought, 'Yeah, that's a nice sentiment but it doesn't feel like You're with me right now!'

Fast-forward a few years to a couple of weeks after the rubbish skip moment. I was sitting at my desk at home when the phone rang – it was five o'clock in the morning.

'Hello... ?'

'Hello, mate! Is that Carl Beech?' It was a bloke with an Australian accent.

'Yes, this is Beechy.'

'It's Stevie.'

'Who's Stevie?'

'Stevie, from Sydney.'

'Who's Stevie from Sydney?'

'Ah, I was at college with you for a bit... I was just having my quiet time.'

'I wondered why you were calling me at five in the morning!'

'No, it's in the evening here.'

'Oh, yeah,' I said.

'I thought I'd phone you... I dug your number out.'

'Why's that?'

'I'm having this prayer time and I felt the Holy Spirit say to me to phone Carl Beech in Essex and tell him that God says He'll never leave him nor forsake him.'

I nearly cried. 'You're kidding me!?'

'No, mate. Anyway, that's all I've got to say, see you later.' And with that, he put the phone down.

Funny, isn't it? When I look back over my thirty-odd years of pursuing God, even through the crushing times,

I can see God's hand at work.

One of my favourite things to do is to shut myself away and paint (surprising, I know!). Recently I painted a large impression of a certain cluster of stars called the Eagle Nebula. It's a truly beautiful sight. If you get the chance, have a look at the famous photograph of it: 'Pillars of Creation'. You'll see these sort of wispy bits that look like little fingers. Except they aren't little; they are up to 40 trillion miles tall! And they are, in essence, star factories. From these pillars of gas and dust, stars are being born. To put it in a little more perspective, these finger-like pillars are said to be bigger than our solar system. That's right – it is huge. And in comparison, we are very, very small.

I don't know about you, but this challenges me. I want to try to understand the mystery of how God can make something so astonishingly big and majestic, and yet also make me. And more than that, He loves me, knows me and has a plan for me.

Let me ask you a question that I also ask myself: do we honestly believe that the God who can make the Eagle Nebula can't take care of the stuff we get angst ridden and stressed about in our lives? Do we honestly believe that God can't take care of our kids, our household issues, our career, our ministry? So often we get numbed and blunted in our pursuit of Christ because we worry or lose sight of God in the mess and stress. But I believe with all my heart that the God who made the universe has got my life in His hands. And your life too! Do you believe it? Do your actions and thoughts demonstrate that belief?

Life can throw all kinds challenges and turmoil our way. We are engaged in battle, but we can have peace knowing that we've got Christ on our side and the power of the Holy Spirit within us. The God who made the Eagle Nebula is for us and within us! So even when we're flapping and it's all terrible, we can take a deep breath and stay calm because God's got us. I'm convinced that one day we will look back on today and say, 'Wow, that was a bit of a ride, wasn't it? It's amazing how God has worked through the pain and the challenges.'

Thank You, God.

'Why do you look at the speck of sawdust in your brother's eye and pay no attention to the plank in your own eye?'

MATTHEW 7:3

Thirteen

They're called blind spots

I like change. For me it's an essential part of living a fulfilled life. I'm not a man of routine. I've never liked the status quo and things becoming too familiar. It's just the way I'm wired. While it's true that I've only been employed by two organisations in the last 20 years, I've survived because things kept changing – or perhaps it was that I kept changing things myself!

I also like things to keep moving around me. I'm not one for long meetings. Anything more than 30 minutes and I start to feel agitated, with an increasing desire to become mischievous, start cracking jokes or poke my eyes to try to stay focused.

I also lose things on a regular basis. I usually have no idea where my keys, wallet, phone, dog, cat, kids or shoes are. I put it down to the fact that I'm a genius whose mind is focused on other things. Karen disputes this profusely. In fact, she says that this can all add up to being somewhat annoying. I, of course, prefer to think of it as endearing.

But then, I once found these notes from my wife to my new PA at work: 'Warning: Carl is prone to moments of panic when he will believe that he has forever lost his keys, wallet, phone – or some other catastrophe has befallen him. The temptation will be to panic as well, but it is imperative you stay calm in these situations as they ALWAYS resolve themselves. I normally slink away and wait until the storm has passed.'

'Hmm, that's fair,' I thought to myself. It gave the office team a good laugh but it also had another effect. You see, until I read that and saw the knowing looks on my friends' and colleagues' faces, I hadn't really noticed that I did this at all.

In fact, I hadn't really noticed that I was a fidget until Karen went on to tell me that as well (backed up by my two daughters). They also proceeded to tell me that if I'm focused on something, I don't hear or see anything around me at all. I disputed that until recently, when I was in the staff car park after speaking at an event. I popped out of the car at the barrier and pressed the intercom to get the attendant in the office to open the barrier. Staring intently at the intercom button waiting for someone to answer, I totally failed to notice that the barrier had opened the second I had pressed the buzzer – and I also failed to hear my three colleagues shouting at me that the barrier was open.

They're called blind spots, and we all have them. We can't see them until someone painfully points them out to us. But see them we must, lest we go through life blindly leaving a trail of destruction behind us. That's why Jesus told us to look at the plank in our own eye before we point out the speck of dust in someone else's.

So here's a challenge for you: ask your closest friends, colleagues and relatives what they think your blind spots are. Go on, I dare you. You may not be able to remove that plank overnight, but at least knowing it's there might make living with you that little bit easier for people!

'Ask and it will be given to you;
seek and you will find;
knock and the door
will be opened to you.'

MATTHEW 7:7

Fourteen

Lost and found
— Nick Shahlavi

I want to share Nick's remarkable story with you. At his lowest point, when a lifestyle of drugs and crime had spiralled out of control, God intervened and turned his life around. Nick sought God and found Him, and I hope his story encourages you to do the same...

My parents split up when I was about two. My dad, who was from Iran, was involved in my life very little, so my mum did her best to raise me. We moved around a lot on the outskirts of Manchester. When I was 15, we moved down south, which is when my life really went downhill. I made friends with the wrong crowd. I started smoking a lot of cannabis, and because of the drugs, I couldn't focus at school and was expelled twice. Then, at 17, I failed my college course and was selling weed to support my addiction to crack cocaine. I was just lost.

I got caught in a bad situation with a lot of older drug dealers. They were robbed and I was wrongly blamed for it. Eventually, I had a threat put on my life. I was petrified – I was dealing with grown men who had done horrible things. I had no father figure around, and I guess this all contributed to my deteriorating mental health. I was at a point where I couldn't see any other way out than ending my life.

At that time, I asked God to help me. It was the first time I'd prayed with all sincerity for God to intervene. But afterwards I felt no different, and I thought I'd blown it.

After that, I made a number of attempts on my life. But many weird things happened that meant I survived them – a sharp hunting knife went as blunt as a butter knife; a deadly amount of painkillers had zero effect. I even started swallowing a cup of rat poison when a friend walked in.

On my way home from a chemist with a bag of needles and syringes that I was planning to harm myself with, the same friend saw me and begged me to get into his car. Later, as I was sitting in the car, this big guy knocked on the door and said he'd fix my situation with the other drug dealers. He told me he knew I didn't have anything to do with the robbery.

I knew something was going on spiritually. God had brought me to a place to hear a message I didn't know I was going to hear. The timing of it all, knowing what I was about to do, showed me God was real and that He loved me. I didn't know anything about the Christian faith but I finally knew purpose. There was a reason for my life and I actually felt special. So, I went home and threw the needles in the bin. I knew for the first time in my life that God had done a miracle.

I knew I needed to get away from that area, so I moved back to Manchester and started going to church. But after a while I got pulled away and back into selling drugs. By this time I was in my twenties. I knew that God was real, but my addiction was eating me up.

Then, one day I got invited to hear a preacher at my mum's church. At the end of his message he invited people who wanted to ask God into their life to come forward. I hesitated, and then the preacher asked if there was a Nick in the room. I froze with fear. I couldn't believe what was happening. I told him that was my name, and he called me forward. He said, 'God knew you in your mother's womb and there's a purpose for your life.' At that moment, I had a flashback to when God saved me as a lost 17-year-old boy and I thought, 'This is nuts. This isn't happening!'

So, I gave my life to Jesus. That same preacher spent time in the coming months discipling me. He showed me I was a new person in Christ. The old was gone; the new had come. If I could focus to see myself now as God sees me, things would change. Once a week I went to church, and after the service he would show me scriptures. After a few months I eventually stopped selling drugs.

I felt like I'd been sleeping for 25 years and I was suddenly awake! I had to tell everyone about this God. I joined a team that went into a prison to share the gospel, as well as a new music-based mission team called Vital Signs. We target the hardest to reach people, who are going through what I went through. We perform songs with a message of transformation, salvation and deliverance. As well as performing, we tell our stories and share the gospel.

We've impacted many people by the grace of God, and are seeing people give their lives to Jesus and being filled with the Holy Spirit.

What motivates me to reach these people is the truth that I now know. I see injustice all over the world with the devil robbing people. I see a price that's been paid for them, to restore them into relationship with God and find purpose. I see that everyone has worth. No man saved me in my situation. It was God Himself that led me to Him, but He's used people to build me up. And so I want to do the same. I don't do it because I have to, but because I have a desire and a passion to. It's part of my newfound purpose.

'Therefore everyone who hears
these words of mine and puts
them into practice is like a wise man
who built his house on the rock.
The rain came down,
the streams rose, and the winds
blew and beat against that house;
yet it did not fall, because it had
its foundation on the rock.'

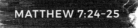

MATTHEW 7:24-25

Fifteen

The way
— every day

Let's note how Jesus concludes His Sermon on the Mount. He says that when we not only hear His teaching but act on it, we are like a wise person who built their house on the rock. Stable and secure... no matter what life throws our way. So let's put everything we have read in Matthew into action.

Here are some counter-cultural daily choices for you to put into practice (inspired by Romans 12:9–21)...

- Be inconvenienced by people joyfully and practise hospitality
- Lace your words with kindness
- Give people the benefit of the doubt
- Practise outrageous generosity
- Lend without expecting back
- Only complain constructively and gracefully – ask yourself, 'Is it even worth it?'
- Say 'Thank you'
- Lose an argument every so often – it's good for you!
- Associate with people who aren't 'like you' and who challenge you
- Listen more
- Honour and prefer others above yourself
- If you find yourself feeling jealous of someone, say genuine nice things about them publicly
- Do humble things
- Take advice and feedback well
- Make kind gestures
- Praise people
- Forgive people
- Pray for people

Sixteen

The way
— online

It's astonishing to me how people who love Jesus, are filled with His Spirit and read their Bibles, can fall into the trap of becoming someone very different online. Let's not be that person. Let the light of Christ shine through your online life and may our offline lives do just the same. Here are my rules for navigating social media as a follower of the way...

- Never criticise people
- Don't deal in hearsay
- Say what you are for, not what you are against
- Take arguments offline. Resolve them quickly
- Don't escalate rows
- Don't use inflammatory rhetoric
- Don't tag people into personally insulting tweets or posts
- Don't assume celebrities are 'fair game'
- Don't ignore people when they reach out to you
- Be gracious
- Apologise when you need to
- Don't respond to antagonism
- Overlook an insult
- Don't obsess about how many 'likes' you have
- Take a break from it every so often and focus on face-to-face interaction
- Don't be crude
- Don't use foul language
- Characterise everything with joy
- Don't share things privately that you wouldn't share publicly
- Have some accountability to what you are posting
- Don't have secret social media accounts
- Don't talk about people online as if they don't exist
- Ask yourself, 'Does my online persona match my offline persona?'

A declaration of
the way

As we come to the end of our look at the way, let's reflect on the following words and take them to heart...

Be known in this life for the way you give,
not the way you take.

Live generously in word and deed.

If you lend anything, do it as if you will never get back what you lent.

Travel lightly through life, holding nothing material too tightly.

Be known for being a person of justice, not blind to the needs of the world.

Be compassionate.

Be kind to your fellow man; make mercy and justice your travelling companions.

Seek to do what is good, resist evil, and never allow hatred of people to take root in your life.

Only hate and despise that which imprisons people's hearts.

Love your family and treasure your moments together.

Spend more time with people.

Always give people the benefit of the doubt and believe the best.

Be prepared to get hurt; walk humbly and live vulnerably.

Keep your heart soft and never let it harden – or the enemy wins.

Work hard, but don't make work your master.

Leader or follower, you are a servant.

Whatever you do, you do before an audience of one.

Be diligent, honest and respectful; be known as a man or woman who finishes the task.

Listen and take criticism and advice well, or you'll fall into error.

One day you'll breathe your last breath, so live life in readiness for the final journey.

Keep God close, and walk in repentance before Him.

Make sure you are at peace with all people.

Point others to the place where you are heading.

When the time comes, you will receive a faith hero's welcome.

Keep on **the way**

Bible reading notes designed to inspire your life every day

With seven different titles of daily Bible reading notes for adults, young people and children to choose from, there is something for everyone.

The adult range includes Selwyn Hughes' renowned *Every Day with Jesus*, the multi-authored, fresh and insightful *Inspiring Women Every Day* and Jeff Lucas' popular, down to earth *Life Every Day*.

Our vibrant range for children and young people (ages 7 to 18) provides daily insights into God's Word and helps readers discover the Bible for themselves.

Choose your way of engaging with God's Word as you receive encouragement to enrich your life every day.

To find out more and to order, visit **www.cwr.org.uk/subscriptions**

How stable is your spiritual life?

This classic from one of the recent Spirirtual Fathers of the UK – Selwyn Hughes – has impacted the lives of hundreds of thousands. Described by Selwyn as the culmination of his life's work, he invites you to learn to depend on Jesus as your source of stability, power and life.

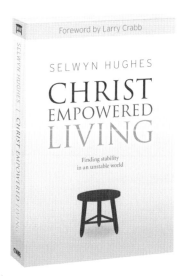

Christ Empowered Living is also available as a resource pack, which includes a workbook and an eight-session DVD for group or individual use.

ISBN: 978-1-85345-201-7

To find out more and to order, visit **www.cwr.org.uk/store**

Courses and seminars

Waverley Abbey College

Publishing and media

Conference facilities

Transforming lives

CWR's vision is to enable people to experience personal transformation through applying God's Word to their lives and relationships.

Our Bible-based training and resources help people around the world to:
- Grow in their walk with God
- Understand and apply Scripture to their lives
- Resource themselves and their church
- Develop pastoral care and counselling skills
- Train for leadership
- Strengthen relationships, marriage and family life and much more.

Our insightful writers provide daily Bible reading notes and other resources for all ages, and our experienced course designers and presenters have gained an international reputation for excellence and effectiveness.

CWR's Training and Conference Centres in Surrey and East Sussex, England, provide excellent facilities in idyllic settings – ideal for both learning and spiritual refreshment.

CWR Applying God's Word to everyday life and relationships

CWR, Waverley Abbey House,
Waverley Lane, Farnham,
Surrey GU9 8EP, UK

Telephone: **+44 (0)1252 784700**
Email: **info@cwr.org.uk**
Website: **www.cwr.org.uk**

Registered Charity No. 294387
Company Registration No. 1990308